Babe Ruth: A Daughter's Portrait

Babe Ruth

A Daughter's Portrait

George Beim

with Julia Ruth Stevens

TAYLOR PUBLISHING COMPANY
DALLAS, TEXAS

Published by Taylor Publishing Company
1550 West Mockingbird Lane
Dallas, Texas 75235

Book design by Mark McGarry
Set in Goudy & Goudy Handtooled

Library of Congress Cataloging-in-Publication Data
Beim, George.
Babe Ruth : a daughter's portrait / George Beim with Julia Ruth Stevens.
p. cm.
ISBN 0-8783-995-7
1. Ruth, Babe, 1895–1948—Pictorial works. 2. Baseball players—United States—
Biography. 3. Baseball players—United States—Biography—Pictorial works.
4. Stevens, Julia Ruth. I. Stevens, Julia Ruth. II. Title.
GV865.R8B45   1998
796.357′092—dc21
[B]   98–9548
CIP

Printed in the United States of America
10 9 8 7 6 5 4 3 2 1

To the five women who are "My Life":

My wife and "partner" Caterina,
and the best children anyone could ever hope for:
Kim, Pam, Beth, and Heather.
Thanks for putting up with me —
"I love you!"

Contents

Introduction

THIS BOOK IS A CONCEPT DEVELOPED BY THE AUTHOR and the late Claire Hodgson Ruth, Babe's wife. The two thought that the public would enjoy being able to see photographs of the Babe from the family albums and other sources that show George Herman Ruth, Jr., the individual, rather than Babe Ruth the baseball player. The intent was to let people see the life of Babe Ruth in pictures. Unfortunately, Claire died before she and the author had an opportunity to embark upon the project. The idea was shelved until the author met Julia Ruth Stevens, the Babe's daughter.

Through the gracious cooperation of this wonderful lady, Julia Ruth Stevens, this book finally became a reality. It is designed to give the public a view of Babe Ruth through the eyes of his daughter and provide a glimpse into the private life of "The Greatest Baseball Player of All Time." Relying on the adage that "a picture is worth a thousand words," we hope that through this book people are able to gain an understanding of what a truly fine and caring person this man was. This publication is also designed to serve as a tribute to George Herman Ruth, Jr., "The Babe," in the year, 1998, that commemorates the 50th anniversary of his death in 1948.

A large portion of the photographs in this book are from the private collection of Julia Ruth Stevens. However, in order to provide a more complete view of "The Babe" other sources were also utilized. We would like to thank all those who assisted in the compilation of the photographs, including The Babe Ruth Museum, The National Baseball Hall of Fame and Linda Ruth Tosseti. In particular we would like to acknowledge the assistance received from Gregory Schwalenberg, curator at the Babe Ruth Museum, for his invaluable assistance. Not only did he assist in this project, but his congeniality and hospitality when we visited the museum were most appreciated.

We strongly recommend anyone who has an interest in "The Babe" to visit The Babe Ruth Museum, located on the site of his birth at 216 Emory Street in Baltimore, Maryland, near Camden Yards. There is an abundance of memorabilia to see, and most of the photographs in this book will now also be available for duplication at the museum.

GEORGE BEIM

Babe Ruth

A Daughter's Portrait

CHAPTER I

The Formative Years

On February 6, 1895, Kate Schamberger Ruth, at the age of nineteen, gave birth to her first child. George Herman Ruth, Jr., was born in the house of his grandparents at 216 Emory Street in Baltimore, Maryland. He was the first of eight children born to Kate and George Herman Ruth. Unfortunately, most of the children died in infancy, and only George, Jr., and his sister Mamie survived to lead a full life.

George Herman Ruth, who worked as a bartender and ultimately opened his own tavern, was only twenty-three at the time of his first son's birth. Both he and his wife worked long hours and spent little time with their son. Subsequently, young George, Jr., spent the first years of his life in a saloon on the Baltimore riverfront. Contrary to popular belief, young George was not an orphan. For the first seven years of his life he was with his parents, but he survived without guidance on the dirty, crowded streets of

"Daddy was born at 216 Emory Street in Baltimore, Maryland, on February 6, 1895. In the photograph his home is the second door from the left. The window directly above the door is from the bedroom in which he was born."

the Baltimore riverfront—stealing from shops, throwing rocks and rotten eggs at delivery truck drivers, running away from police and basically being on his own.

Young George experienced little, if any, real love from his parents who made no time for their son. Ultimately, they felt that they could no longer care for their son and on June 13, 1902, George Herman Ruth took his seven year old to St. Mary's Industrial School for Boys. Not only did he place young George in the school, but he signed over custody of the boy to the Xaverian Brothers, a Catholic Order of Jesuit Missionaries who ran St. Mary's.

St. Mary's was both a reformatory and orphanage, which was surrounded by a wall similar to a prison with guards on duty. There were approximately 800 children at St. Mary's, which had four dormitories that housed about 200 kids each. George, Jr., who by the age of seven had already been involved with mischievous altercations, was classified as "incorrigible" upon his admission. Although for a few brief periods he was returned to live with his family, he was always sent back to St. Mary's. It was a hard way for a youngster to grow up. No one ever came to visit him while he was at St. Mary's, not on the one Sunday per month that visitors were allowed, not on holidays, nor even at Christmas.

Perhaps the one positive thing stemming from his time at St. Mary's was meeting Brother Mathias. A big and intimidating man, some six feet six inches tall, Brother Matthias was the main disciplinarian at St. Mary's. He spent a great deal of time with George, Jr., providing the guidance and support that the youngster did not receive from his parents. He even helped young Ruth develop as a baseball player. It is because of his difficult childhood and the positive influence of Brother Mathias that Babe Ruth came to love children and why all of his life he went out of his way to do things for kids, especially those in need.

Baseball was a popular and primary form of recreation for the boys at St. Mary's and young George Ruth, Jr., displayed his potential at a young age. He played all positions on the field, was an excellent pitcher and certainly had the ability to hit the ball. By his late teens Babe Ruth had developed into a major league baseball prospect. On February 27, 1914, at the age of nineteen, Ruth was signed to his first professional baseball contract by Jack Dunn, manager of the Baltimore Orioles, at the time a minor league franchise in the International League. Because George, Jr.'s parents had signed over custody of the youngster to St. Mary's he was supposed to remain at the school until the age of twenty-one. To circumvent this Dunn became Ruth's legal guardian.

Jack Dunn was well-known for picking up youngsters whom he thought had major league potential. When George Ruth, Jr., appeared with Dunn at the ballpark the other players started cracking jokes, and one of the players quipped, "Well, here's Jack's newest Babe." The rest of the players also started referring to young George as "Babe" and the name stuck. Thus began the storied career of Babe Ruth.

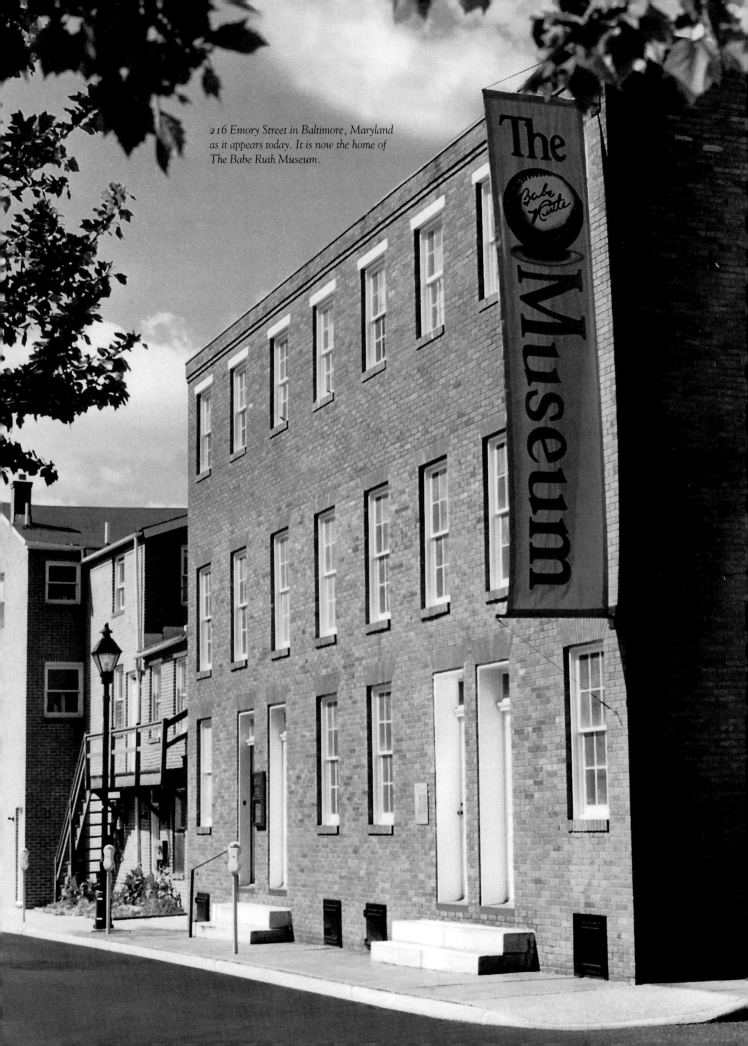

216 Emory Street in Baltimore, Maryland as it appears today. It is now the home of The Babe Ruth Museum.

The Babe Ruth Museum

"Daddy and his mother are the first ones on the left, and his father is sitting on the step (also in the front row) smoking a long-stemmed pipe, wearing a straw hat, bow tie and vest. This is the only photograph that I've ever seen of Daddy and both of his parents at the same time."

"Daddy (2nd from left) and his father (right), George Herman Ruth, in the Baltimore tavern that his father owned and operated. I continue to be amazed at the remarkable resemblance of Daddy and his father. Daddy bought the bar for his father and forgave him for all the years he never visited Daddy while he was growing up at St. Mary's."

Mary Margaret Ruth Moberly (August 2, 1900 - July 1, 1992) "Mamie and Daddy were the only children from their family who did not die in infancy. She had a twin sister who was one of the six Ruth children who died at an early age."

"Daddy in 1898 at the age of three."

"St. Mary's Industrial School for Boys was Daddy's home from the age of seven until he was signed by the Baltimore Orioles at the age of nineteen."

"The main entrance to St. Mary's. It was really as much a reformatory as it was an orphanage."

"Brother Mathias had a profound positive influence on Daddy while he was at St. Mary's. Daddy admired and respected him greatly."

"*Daddy at the age of sixteen playing shortstop. At St. Mary's he played in the infield, the outfield, was a catcher and of course became an outstanding pitcher.*"

George Herman Ruth, Jr. (with catcher's mask and mitt, center of last row, in a St. Mary's team picture) "He liked being a catcher, but since they didn't have a left hander's catcher's mitt Daddy had to use a right hander's mitt as you can see in the photograph."

"The playground at St. Mary's where Daddy learned to play baseball."

"Daddy at St. Mary's."

"*Daddy loved to dress well and took great pride in how he looked, even when he was young.*"

"*Even when sporting a tie, a bat was never far from his reach.*"

"Daddy with one of the Xaverian Brothers at St. Mary's."

"He was a natural in front of the camera from the outset."

"At the age of nineteen, Daddy signed his first professional baseball contract. It was with the Baltimore Orioles, who at that time were a minor league team in the International League."

RUTH
PITCHER

INTERNATIONAL

CHAPTER 2

Family Memories

JUST FIVE MONTHS AFTER BEING SIGNED BY THE
Baltimore Orioles, Babe Ruth was sold to the Boston Red Sox.
He made his debut as a major leaguer in Fenway Park on July
11, 1914, pitching against the Cleveland Indians.

In the mornings Ruth would frequent Landers' Coffee Shop in Boston, and it is
here that he met Helen Woodford, a seventeen-year-old waitress. Just a few months
later, they got married on October 17, 1914 at St. Paul's Roman Catholic Church in
Ellicott City, Maryland. As Babe's career began to blossom and his salary increased, by
1919 he was making $10,000 per year, he and Helen were able to buy a home outside
of Boston in Sudbury, Massachusetts. The couple was married for fifteen years, but in
truth they were happy and together for only the first few years.

In December of 1919 Babe was sold to the New York Yankees, owned by Colonel
Jacob Ruppert and managed by Miller Huggins. Prior to Ruth's arrival in New York
the team had never won a pennant. With "The Babe" as part of their arsenal they

became a dominant force in major league baseball, winning seven pennants and four World Championships from 1920 to 1933.

In New York, Babe and Helen moved into the Ansonia Hotel on Broadway, which was also the New York home for many celebrities. Unlike her husband, Helen was shy and reserved and did not enjoy the constant notoriety that accompanied Babe wherever he went. As a result, she preferred staying at their rural home outside of Boston, where they had a farm with some 200 acres of land and privacy.

As his popularity and celebrity status grew, Babe was increasingly called away from home. Helen was by herself for lengthy periods of time and their marriage suffered. In 1921 they adopted a baby girl, Dorothy. However, even their mutual love for the child was not sufficient impetus to help strengthen their marriage, which by most accounts was in shambles by 1925 when they formally separated. Neither Babe nor Helen wished to terminate their marriage through divorce because of religious convictions, but for all intent and purposes they were no longer living as man and wife for several years prior to their formal separation.

On January 11, 1929, at the age of 31, Helen died of suffocation in a fire at the Watertown, Massachusetts, house where she was living at the time. For a number of years she had been living with Dr. Edward H. Kinder, a dentist in Watertown. It was his house that burned, due to some defective electrical wiring. Dorothy, who was eight years old at the time was away at boarding school.

In 1923 Babe met and became seriously interested in an attractive and intelligent young widow, Claire Hodgson. Claire had come to New York from Georgia with her young daughter Julia in 1920 and worked as a model and actress with small parts in films and on stage. Although Babe and Claire fell in love, they were not free to marry until Helen's tragic death. On April 17, 1929, the two were finally married in St. Gregory the Great Roman Catholic Church in New York. This was the day before the Opening Day Game against the Boston Red Sox at Yankee Stadium on April 18, and as a wedding present to Claire Babe hit a home run in his first at bat.

In October 1930 Babe formally adopted Claire's daughter Julia, who was thirteen at the time, while Claire did the same with Dorothy who was nine. For the first few years of their marriage the couple resided in an eleven room apartment, which took up the seventh floor of the building on 345 West 88th Street in New York. They next moved to 173 Riverside Drive and in 1942 made their final move to an eleven room apartment at 110 Riverside Drive.

"Daddy made his debut as a major league baseball player for the Boston Red Sox in Fenway Park on July 11, 1914. He pitched seven innings and was credited with the win in a 4 - 3 game."

(L - R) Babe, Helen Woodford Ruth (His first wife), and Bill Joyce. After marrying Helen Woodford, in 1914, Babe and his new wife first lived in a cottage at Willis Pond in Sudbury, Massachusetts, owned by Bill Joyce.

George Herman Ruth, Jr., at Willis Pond in 1915.

Babe and Helen Ruth purchased a 200 acre farm with a large house in Sudbury, Massachusetts. After Babe signed with the New York Yankees they kept their Sudbury home, and Helen really preferred the rural privacy to the constant notoriety that surrounded them in New York City.

Babe Ruth's former home in Sudbury, Massachusetts, as it looked during the Christmas Season in 1988.

*Helen Woodford Ruth and Dorothy, the daughter she and Babe
adopted as an infant in 1921.*

Helen Woodford Ruth is laid to rest after her tragic death. She suffocated in a fire at the house where she was living on January 11, 1929, at the age of 31. (L - R) Third person from the left (in front) is Helen Woodford's sister Josephine, Babe, and Helen's mother Joanna.

"Mother (Claire Hodgson Ruth) and Daddy just before their wedding on April 17, 1929. Mother was trying to get used to all the publicity that surrounded them. They had hoped to avoid a lot of publicity by getting married before 6 a. m., but the public and the media turned out anyway."

"George and Marie Lovell were in attendance on Mother and Daddy's wedding day."

"The newlyweds at their wedding breakfast."

"After the wedding, Mother and Daddy came back to
the apartment at 345 West 88th Street in New York
City."

"Mother gives Daddy a kiss on their wedding day."

"Daddy makes believe that he is tasting mother's cooking for the photographers. Actually, mother did not like to cook. She had a housekeeper and spent as little time as possible in the kitchen."

"They certainly made a handsome and happy couple."

"Since the baseball season started the day after their wedding, Mother and Daddy had to delay their honeymoon. Here they are having fun on the beach during their honeymoon at Palm Beach, Florida in 1930."

"They may have had to wait to go on their honeymoon, but once they got to Florida they had a wonderful time."

"Mother and Daddy back home in New York."

"*Daddy reads some of the letters and cards from his many fans to Mother.*"

"Mother and Daddy enjoying a quiet evening at home with Mother playing the piano."

"Daddy and I relaxing. Wasn't he a handsome and dapper man?"

"Mother and I are glancing over Daddy's shoulders as he holds the newspaper. Actually, Daddy didn't read much because he was afraid it would damage his eyes. As a result, Mother used to read books and magazines to him. Daddy also rarely went to the movies for the same reason."

"Mother and Daddy are all smiles as they look over his new $80,000 per year contract that he signed in March of 1930 with the New York Yankees. That was certainly a tremendous amount of money in those days."

(L - R) Claire, Dorothy, Julia, and Babe "In October of 1930 Mother adopted Dorothy and Daddy formally adopted me. Now we were really a family!"

(L - R) Julia, Babe, Dorothy, and Claire "That certainly looks like a happy family to me."

(L - R) Dorothy, Claire, Babe, and Julia "We were very lucky to be able to travel a fair amount with Daddy. Here we are leaving on a trip in January of 1931."

"Off to Florida, in February of 1932, for some golf and then spring training in St. Petersburg."

(L - R) Claire, Julia, and Babe "It was always a wonderful experience to come to Yankee Stadium for a World Series game. Of course, they always decorated Yankee Stadium for the World Series games and for Opening Day."

"Daddy loved to clown around. Here we are in Artie McGovern's Gym, with Daddy taking time out from his training to fool around with me. That's Artie in the background."

(L - R) Julia, Dorothy, Claire, and Babe *"February 6, 1933, we celebrated Daddy's 38th birthday. One of his fans sent him a fantastic cake, which was a replica of Yankee Stadium. It even had a tiny figure, resembling Daddy, standing at home plate."*

(L - R) Babe and Claire with Lyn and Mary Lary *"Mother and Daddy with their friends Lyn and Mary Lary. Lyn was an infielder for the Yankees and Mary was a movie and stage actress better known as Mary Lawler."*

(L - R) Julia, Claire, and Babe "Opening Day at Yankee Stadium was always exciting. Here Daddy poses for photographs before the start of the first game of the 1933 season."

"Lake Oscawana, New York, was a wonderful place where we would spend that rare day off, during the summer, with family and friends."

Julia Ruth Stevens at Lake Oscawana, New York in August of 1933.

"Daddy horsing around with me at the lake. He would do anything for a laugh. Mother was watching us from the porch and getting a big kick out of it all."

"Mother, Dorothy, and me with Daddy looking on from the porch at the lake."

(L - R) Lefty and June Gomez, Claire, Babe, and Dorothy on the porch "Lefty Gomez and his wife June were good friends of the family and often spent time with Mother and Daddy."

"It's been a wonderful day, but now we have to pack up and head for home. Daddy certainly isn't thrilled about that prospect. That's my grandmother in the background."

"Mother, Daddy and I went to see the Yankees play the Washington Senators on June 20, 1935. It was Daddy's first public appearance since he quit playing for the Boston Braves."

"Mother, Daddy, and I in 1934 right after my high school graduation from Tisne Institute. Daddy was playing in St. Louis and the team was taking a train back to New York. Even though he wasn't supposed to fly, since it wasn't considered that safe back then, he caught a flight back anyway. I guess he figured forgiveness would be easier to get from Colonel Ruppert (Yankees owner) and Miller Huggins (Yankees Manager) than permission. The plane was late and he almost missed my graduation."

"Daddy and me at Lido Beach Country Club on Long Island, New York, during July of 1936. This is one of my favorite photographs"

"I was no great shakes at the piano, but once in a while I'd try to play and Daddy would join in. That was always fun."

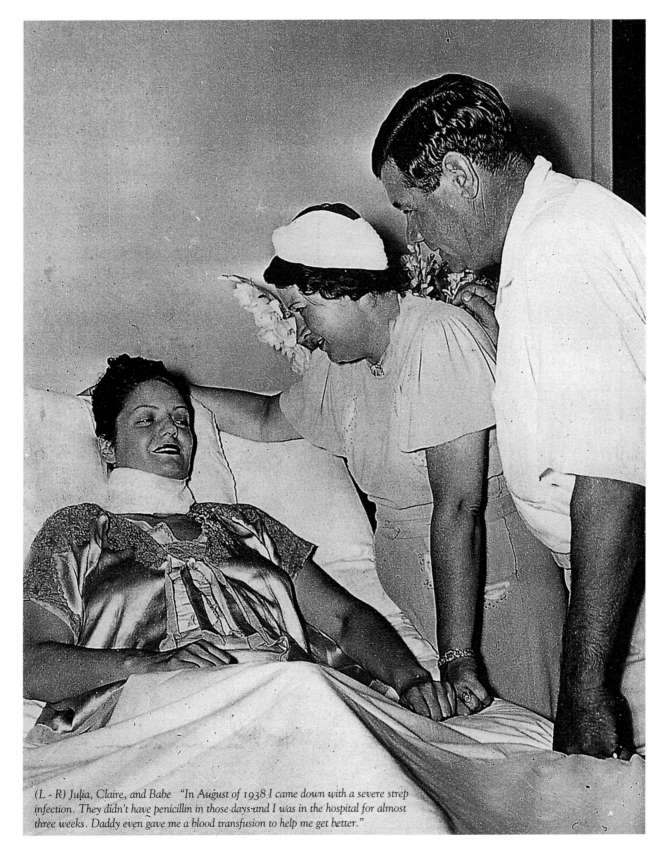

(L - R) Julia, Claire, and Babe "In August of 1938 I came down with a severe strep infection. They didn't have penicillin in those days and I was in the hospital for almost three weeks. Daddy even gave me a blood transfusion to help me get better."

"It was February 24, 1940 and we were off on another trip."

"This was one of the proudest moments of my life. It was the day Daddy walked me down the aisle to wed Richard Wells Flanders on May 1, 1940, in New York."

"Daddy laying down the law to my husband Richard at our wedding reception. He figured the baseball bat would work better than a rolling pin."

"This is the bedroom of the last apartment Daddy lived in at 110 Riverside Drive in New York City. The apartment had a total of eleven rooms."

"Looking out at the Outer Drive, by the Hudson River, from the room in the apartment at 110 Riverside Drive where Daddy spent a lot of time listening to the radio."

56

"Daddy was just a spectator at this game, but people still wanted to take pictures and say hello."

April of 1947 at Yankee Stadium. "People really loved to see Daddy at games, even if he was no longer playing."

"Daddy was the light of my life. I loved him very much. You know, he was an excellent dancer and I really preferred dancing with him than with any of my dates."

"Mother and Daddy in Los Angeles in May of 1948. Daddy was helping with the filming of 'The Babe Ruth Story.'"

"Mother and Daddy leaving Los Angeles on their way back to New York in May of 1948."

"Daddy did a lot of traveling for American Legion Baseball, even while he was sick. Here he and mother are taking off for another appearance."

(L - R) Julia, Maime Ruth Moberly, Claire, and Brooks Robinson at Brooks Robinson's restaurant in Baltimore, Maryland in 1970.

CHAPTER 3

The Sportsman

HAD BABE RUTH BEEN BORN FIFTY YEARS LATER he would unquestionably have been a star in several sports, at least as a youngster. However, at the time of his youth baseball was basically the only true "sport of choice." Nevertheless, the Babe was interested in almost all sporting activities and participated in most of them. He had a passion for hunting and fishing, boxed, bowled, and would try pretty much any sport.

Perhaps one of his biggest athletic passions was golf. He loved the game and played whenever he could. As a matter of fact, his daughter Julia still believes that were it not for golf he would not have known what to do with himself after he retired from baseball.

"This was an oil painting of Daddy that used to hang in our game room. After he died it went to the Baseball Hall of Fame in Cooperstown. He was really an excellent athlete and not only enjoyed but was also good at most sports."

"While playing with Boston, in the beginning of his career, Daddy was really the best left-handed pitcher in baseball. However, he was also a great hitter and once he joined the Yankees he basically gave up pitching."

"Prior to Daddy joining the New York Yankees they had never won the pennant, but with his powerful bat in their line-up they won seven pennants and four World Championships from 1920 to 1933. The 1927 New York Yankees pictured here are considered by many to be the greatest team in baseball history."

"In March of 1930, Daddy signed a two year contract with the Yankees for $80,000 per year. The average annual player salary at the time was around $7,000. Mother and Colonel Jacob Ruppert, owner of the Yankees, look on as Daddy signs the contract."

"Look at Daddy's face. You just know that this will be another home run."

"In 1933 Daddy met with Colonel Ruppert at the Colonel's brewery to sign a one-year contract for $52,000. It was quite a bit lower than the $75,000 he was paid in 1932, but then the country was in the Depression and about one of every four people were out of work."

"Colonel Jacob Ruppert, owner of the New York Yankees and Daddy."

"Daddy led the league in home runs in twelve seasons and is the all-time leader in the number of home runs per time at bat."

"This is one of those classic photos of Daddy swinging a bat and watching the ball sail into the stands."

"Daddy bowled fairly regularly and really enjoyed it."

"This doesn't look much like a baseball glove, but Daddy would try anything. Here he tries on a cesta, used to catch and propel the ball in jai alai."

"So this is a pelota. That's the ball they use in jai alai and it doesn't look much like a baseball, but Daddy is willing to give it a try."

"Daddy tries his hand at jai alai in the fronton. He really did almost anything for the photographers and to put on a show."

"Bill Tilden, who was a great American tennis player in the twenties, tries to give Daddy some tennis pointers. Daddy was good at so many sports, but he never took up tennis."

"Daddy working out at Artie McGovern's Gym. He actually loved boxing."

"*Most people don't know that Daddy was also a boxing referee. Here he entertains the crowd before the start of a fight.*"

"*Daddy could also shoot a pretty good game of pool. He had a pool table in our apartment on 88th street and often enjoyed a game with friends after dinner*"

"Crochet may not be as demanding as baseball, but Daddy was game for almost anything."

"Fishing was another one of Daddy's loves, especially after he retired. It helped to take his mind off how really miserable he felt being out of baseball."

CHAMBER OF COMME
MIAMI BEACH
DOCKS FLORID

"Not a bad catch. That's Daddy in Miami Beach, Florida, in 1947."

"Hunting was one of Daddy's favorite pastimes."

"Of course Daddy took very good care of his guns. Here he is cleaning them prior to another hunting trip."

"Daddy hunted many different things. The alligator that he shot is a pretty good sized one."

"That's Daddy in the middle, with teammate Herb Pennock on the left, getting ready for an off-season hunting trip in Kenneth Square."

"Herb Pennock is on the first horse and Daddy is on the second, setting out with the hunting dogs."

"Daddy was often invited to go hunting on private preserves."

"Daddy was a skillful hunter and no matter what they were after they usually bagged their fair share."

"How about some pheasant under glass?"

"This one is certainly a big one."

"Well, looks like Mother won't have to go out and buy a turkey for Thanksgiving dinner."

"This time Daddy's prey were geese."

"Even when he was on a hunting trip the kids would find him, and Daddy always made time for them."

"In 1936 Daddy went on a hunting trip to Nova Scotia. Those are Daddy's friends Jack Matthews (slightly crouching) and Bob Edge with Daddy and some others who were helping them after they returned from hunting in the bush."

"Bob Edge and Jack Matthews are the first two on the left and that's Daddy with the deer draped over his shoulders."

(L - R) Bob Edge, Babe, and Jack Matthews "Jack Matthews lived in New York at the time of this trip in 1936 and was married to Anne Elstner, who was Stella Dallas on radio."

"Daddy made a bear skin rug out of this bear and gave it to me.
My husband and I had a ski lodge in New Hampshire and
Daddy felt that the rug would look better there than in New
York City."

"Jack Matthews is sitting on the bear, with Daddy and Bob Edge on the right: a bear, a moose and
several deer, not a bad result from the 1936 Nova Scotia trip."

"The hunters relax after a successful day. (L - R) That's Bob Edge, Daddy, their guide for the hunting trip, and Jack Matthews. Jack had a fish and game show on the radio and arranged the trip to Nova Scotia."

(L - R) Bob Edge, guide, Jack Matthews, and Babe "Daddy also enjoyed playing cards, and loved to play in the evenings after they finished hunting or fishing. He had a fantastic card sense. Even though he did not know the basic rules, he would often sit down to make a fourth at bridge with my girlfriends and me."

"Golf really was one of Daddy's big passions in life. This photo was taken
when he was playing in Hot Springs, Arkansas, during the 20s."

"Notice that Daddy was a real trend setter. He was wearing his cap backwards even back then."

"Daddy was quite good at golf. He even thought about becoming a professional golfer, but by the time he retired from baseball it was really too late to try that."

"He was an excellent amateur golfer."

"That looks like pretty good form to me."

"Even when he was traveling, Daddy found time to get out on the golf course. Here he is playing at the American Golf Club outside of Paris, France, in 1934."

"Another couple of inches and that ball would have dropped in. You can see that Daddy was not too happy with
the result of that putt."

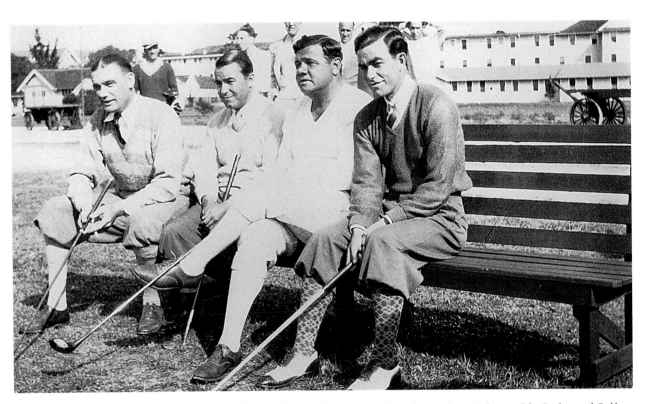

"Waiting to tee it up. (L - R) That's Rube Marquard, Gene Sarazen, the great pro golfer who is a charter inductee of the Professional Golfers
Hall of Fame, Daddy, and Johnny Farrell at Bellair Country Club in Clearwater, Florida."

"Daddy and Bob Brumby at St. Albans Golf Club in April of 1940."

CHAPTER 4

The World Traveler

THE PROWESS OF BABE RUTH SPREAD AROUND THE globe, and due to his accomplishments he was able to travel extensively. Babe and his family visited such places as the Hawaiian Islands, Europe, and the Far East. One of his more memorable trips was to Japan in 1934, when he accompanied a team of major league baseball players from the United States who were invited to play a series of exhibition games. The Japanese adored him. He was as big a hit in the Far East as he was at home.

"In 1933 a public relations man, Herb
Hunter, arranged for Daddy to make a
series of appearances in Hawaii. That's
Herb, on the left next to Daddy, as we
arrived in Honolulu."

(L - R) "That's me with Daddy and Mother arriving in
Honolulu on October 19, 1933. It was a dream for me to go
on the trip, and it was absolutely wonderful."

"Here we are being welcomed by a couple of Hawaiian girls in
grass skirts."

"The man welcoming Daddy was a pure-blooded
Hawaiian."

"Daddy appreciated the warm reception that we received
and was happy to pose with the Hawaiian gentleman and
his wife."

"Mother and I in front of the Royal Hawaiian Hotel
where we stayed. It was really a wonderful place."

"At the beautiful Tea Gardens."

"I took this picture of Daddy with Spencer Tracy at Waikiki just as Daddy decided to scratch his head. Since I didn't want to impose I didn't take another shot of them."

"Daddy and I at the beach at Waikiki. It was simply a marvelous time!"

"In 1934 a team of American major league baseball All-Stars was invited to the Far East to play some exhibition games in Japan and Manila. Mother and I were able to accompany Daddy. After the All-Star Tour was over most of the players and their wives went back home, but we extended our trip to see more of the world. It was our "Trip Around the World.""

L - R) Julia, Babe, and Claire "Daddy, the gay cabalero. Our trip started by train to Vancouver. We had an eight hour lay over in Chicago, so we visited the Worlds Fair. Daddy had a great time and picked up a sombrero for himself as a souvenir."

"Mother, Daddy, and I leaving Vancouver on board the ship Empress of Japan. This was the start of our 'round the world trip."

Julia Ruth Stevens (October, 1934)
"Table tennis was a nice way to pass some time on board ship during our trip. However, as you can see my form left a lot to be desired."

"H. R. Brown (L), of Honolulu, greeted us upon our arrival in Hawaii. (L - R)
That's June Gomez, Daddy, Violet and Earl Whitehill, Mother, and Lefty Gomez.
Earl was a pitcher from Detroit and also a member of the All-Stars."

"Daddy trying to teach me trap shooting. I didn't
take to it very well, but it was always fun to
spend 'quality time' with Daddy."

"We stopped over in Hawaii on the way to Japan. Here are 'Our Boys,' members of the American All-Stars, as we arrived in Hawaii. Daddy
is in the middle of the back row."

(L - R) Babe, Claire, Jimmy Reese, and Julia
"Jimmy Reese was one of Daddy's roommates and a really nice guy. He spent his entire life in baseball as both a player and later a coach."

"When we arrived in Japan the wives of the players were given flowers by our hosts. That's me standing next to Daddy with June Gomez and Elenore Gehrig on my left."

"*All the American All-Stars, and especially Daddy, drew throngs of people wherever they went in Japan. That's Daddy walking with Mother on his arm.*"

"*The American All-Stars pose for a picture at a radio interview in Japan. Daddy is the third from the left in the back row.*"

"The Japanese youngsters adored Daddy, and as always he made it a point to find time for the kids."

"Daddy at a pre-game tea party with two Japanese hostesses."

"They had a caricature of Daddy's face on the cover of the game program in Tokyo. Even all the people in Japan knew what he looked like."

"The American All-Stars before a game in Japan. Besides Daddy, there were a lot of future Hall of Famers on the trip with the team including Lou Gehrig, Charlie Gehringer, Jimmy Foxx, Earl Averill, Lefty Gomez, and Connie Mack."

"Daddy was probably as popular in Japan as he was back home. Wherever he went people swarmed to catch a glimpse of him or perhaps even get an autograph."

(L - R) Julia, Lefty and June Gomez, Babe, and Claire "We stayed in Bali for four days and toured the island. It was the Dutch East Indies back then. The island was primitive but quite beautiful, and the native dancers were fantastic."

(L - R) Front Row: Millie McNair, Julia, Claire, Rose Hillerich, and June Gomez; Back Row: Eric McNair, "Doc" Eldredge, Babe, Bud Hillerich, and Lefty Gomez "Back on board ship. After playing in Manila we left on our 'Trip Around the World.' We stopped in a number of exotic ports, including Bali and Java before arriving in Marseilles, France."

"The pals in Bali, Lefty Gomez and Daddy."

"I really loved traveling with Daddy and seeing all these fascinating places. That's the two of us in Bali."

"June and Lefty Gomez with Mother and Daddy in Bali."

(L - R) Julia, Babe, and Claire "It was quite a hike to get to the top of the temple in Java, so we needed a little rest before going on."

"Our first stop in Europe was Marseilles, the port where we arrived. From Marseilles we travelled by train to Paris where we stayed for ten days. Next we went to St. Moritz. Here we are in front of the Palace Hotel. That's me on the left, Daddy, mother and a local St. Bernard who must have been a baseball fan, but our departure from Paris was delayed because Mother came down with the flu."

"An American and his son vacationing in St. Moritz asked us to have a picture taken with them. In the middle is Van, a man from Holland whom we met on the ship to Marseilles and who was on an extended holiday also going to St. Moritz, Daddy and I are on either side of Van."

"Daddy on his way to do some skiing and Mother. She was recovering from a severe case of flu and didn't try skiing, but Daddy and I did."

"Mother and Daddy in St. Moritz. This could have made a very nice Christmas card photo."

(L - R) Claire, Babe, Julia and Van. "This was actually the only time that Daddy went skiing, but I took it up years later when my husband and I moved to New Hampshire."

(L - R) "Van, Me, Daddy, and Mother with our new St. Bernard friend."

"With our 'Around the World' trip drawing to a close, we flew to London to catch a ship back home. That's me on the left with Daddy and Mother. Mother was only sixteen years older than me and we could probably have passed for sisters."

"Mother, Daddy, and I in front of the
plane we flew to London."

"Daddy waves good-bye with me next to him and Mother to the right. The flight to London was actually the first
time flying for both Mother and me."

(L - R) Claire, Babe, and Julia "We arrived back home from our trip in January of 1935. It was a wonderful time, but there's really no place like home."

CHAPTER 5

The Pied Piper of Kids

PERHAPS IT WAS BECAUSE AS A CHILD HE DID NOT receive the love all children deserve, perhaps it was because his childhood was such a difficult one—being reared in an orphanage/reformatory—or perhaps it was because of something all together different. Regardless of the reason Babe Ruth loved children and children adored Babe Ruth. Wherever he went children flocked to him and he never tried to discourage them from surrounding him. He genuinely loved kids and felt that he had to do whatever he could to help those children who were in need. Although he may not have always enjoyed public appearances, he never turned down a request to visit or help kids. He made countless visits to children in hospitals and orphanages, and always did what was asked of him to help charitable causes associated with children. This even included St. Mary's. He never tried to hide his roots and difficult childhood, and once he became established he did much to help St. Mary's and the Xaverian Brothers who ran it.

One of the more interesting stories about Babe Ruth and children is his encounter with Johnny Sylvester. Young Johnny was seriously ill and not really improving. His father went to see the Babe, told him that the youngster idolized Babe and asked if Babe might come to see Johnny. Ruth went to visit the boy in the hospital to cheer him up, and gave him a bat and an autographed ball. As an incentive for the youngster to get well he told the boy that he would hit a home run just for him that afternoon in Yankee Stadium. Babe kept his promise and young Johnny did indeed get well.

"Daddy genuinely loved children and tried never to turn down requests for him to visit kids in hospitals and orphanages, or help charitable causes for children. Here he is with the children of St. Ann's Home in Tacoma, Washington."

"Daddy would do anything to make children happy. He also loved to clown around for photographers."

"Young Sherwood Gerber got a lifetime memory when he was given the opportunity to meet Daddy at Cominsky Park in 1932."

"Wherever Daddy went he really did attract kids like the Pied Piper. He was the idol of so many children, and they were ecstatic when they had an opportunity to meet and be with him."

"There were not a lot of kids who wouldn't treasure an autograph from Daddy."

"A visit to Presbyterian Hospital in 1939 certainly lifted the spirits of the children who were ill, and that autographed ball will surely be treasured. That's nurse Mildred Wilkins with Daddy."

"Daddy fooling around with kids at Artie McGovern's Gym in January of 1934. He used to work out at the gym before he left for spring training in Florida. That's Artie on the far left."

"Anything to make a child laugh and cheer him up. Daddy didn't
have to speak a child's language in order to make him happy.
He just had a wonderful way with kids."

"Even when leaving on a trip Daddy made time for the children."

"I really believe that being surrounded by children and making them happy brought Daddy joy."

"Happiness is a bunch of smiling young faces."

"Catering to and serving kids was a a chore Daddy undertook most willingly. It was certainly a thrill for the children, even though this little girl doesn't seem to be too sure at the moment."

"Moe Springer, (12) of Chicago, receives a trophy from Daddy for
winning The Miami Biltmore Kids Golf Championship. The other
youngster in the photograph is little Billy Munsell, (6) also of
Chicago, who came in second."

"On March 9, 1935, Daddy was commissioned a major by the
Florida Military Academy in St. Petersburg."

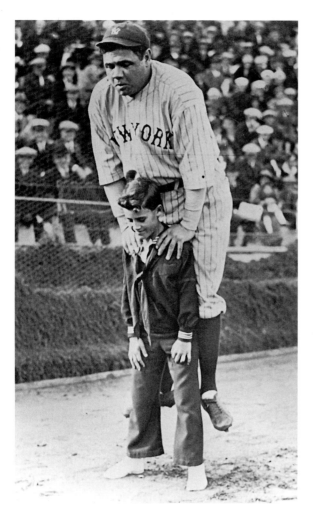

"Horsing around with kids was fun for Daddy."

*"At the World's Fair Court of Sports, on May 31, 1939,
Daddy demonstrates his swing to some of the children."*

"On February 2, 1942, Daddy is welcomed to Los Angeles by the Nazareth Orphan Band."

"When Daddy talked to children he never had any problem keeping their attention."

"An autograph for a boy scout, and the hat on Daddy's head to create a better shot for the photographer."

"You would be cheering too if you got a chance to meet your idol. From the look on Daddy's face he's having a pretty good time too."

"On December 12, 1941, Daddy gave a surprise party for thirty little Infantile Paralysis patients at the Hospital for Joint Diseases in New York. Here he feeds little Marie who was three. He brought baseball bats, toys, ice cream, and cake for the children and spent the day with them."

"Five organizations combined to have the 'official' opening of 'Make It a Case for a Kid' Week on June 14, 1947. It was an effort to have 30,000 pieces of luggage donated to children who were being sent to summer camps by these organizations. Daddy, in our apartment, presented suit cases to some members of the Boys' Club and Salvation Army."

"The sister Kenny Foundation held a Christmas party for children with Infantile Paralysis at the Astor Hotel on December 10, 1947. Even though he was ill at the time, Daddy played Santa Claus for the kids to help cheer them up. About fifty children were at the party, including Jimmy McCall (3) and Jane Greenfield (3 1/2)."

"Little Jimmy McCall (3) gives Daddy a kiss after he received a baseball."

"Young Johnny Every helps taste the cake and celebrate Daddy's 53rd birthday in February of 1948 in Miami Beach, Florida."

"Daddy is holding a bat covered with Easter Seals, while young Russell Samuel, on the left with a ball also covered with Easter Seals, makes believe he is about to pitch the ball. This was on February 27, 1948, when Daddy helped with the start of the Southern District Easter Seal Campaign."

"Could this little guy be the next Babe Ruth? Even when he was ill, being with children brought a smile to Daddy's face."

"Children always wanted to seek Daddy out. He and Mother are returning from Florida on March 28, 1948."

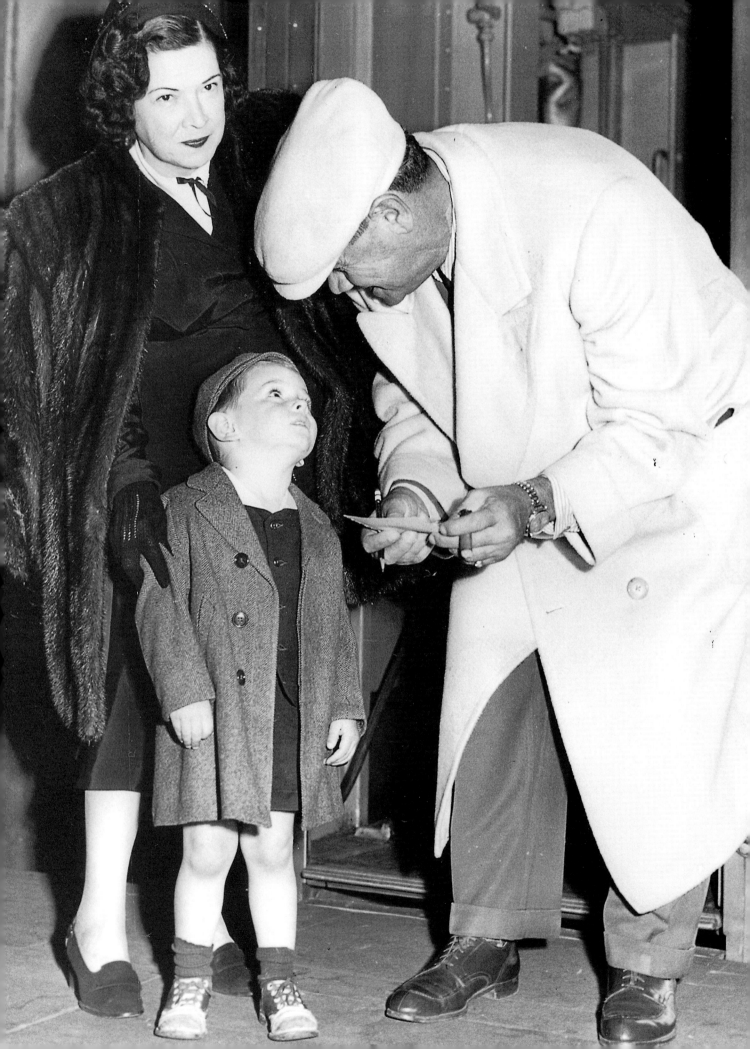

CHAPTER 6

A Photographer's Dream

Babe Ruth enjoyed being photographed and would even go as far as to put on a little "show" to entertain photographers and give them an opportunity to get a great shot. He loved to fool around and often times was caught on camera creating a priceless photograph. He took a lot of pride in dressing well and made a great model for the photographers. Babe was also frequently in the company of other well known celebrities, thus, creating great photo opportunities. Babe knew a photo-op when he saw one.

Babe was also friends with many reporters. Each year he even held a formal dinner for the baseball writers, and not infrequently would invite reporters, along with their wives, to his home for dinner.

"Daddy signs an autograph for Armstead Williams (2 1/2) on April 28, 1948, with Mother standing on the left. The look on little Armstead's face truly exemplifies how children idolized Daddy. I just love this picture."

"Daddy always took great pride in how he looked, and he liked to dress well. After he married Mother, she would often help him pick out fabric for suits and helped to keep him looking good."

"Showing off his new car and raccoon coat, which he wore to football games when it was cold."

"Certainly a dapper looking young man."

*"Daddy in March of 1930 in front of the Menger Hotel in San Antonio,
Texas."*

"Sometimes Daddy did radio broadcasts, as seen in this photo."

"He loved to smoke cigars and appears with one in many photographs."

"This was taken on my wedding day, May 1, 1940, just before Daddy entered the church. It was a wonderful day."

"This is one of my favorite shots of Daddy. It was the way I thought of him, in 'civies' and not in a baseball uniform."

"After retiring from baseball he still really longed to get back into the game. He only wanted to manage at the major league level, but never got the opportunity."

"Daddy was photographed with many famous people. Here he is with Fanny Brice at Bowie Race Track in 1922."

"Miller Huggins, New York Yankees manager, goes for a ride with Daddy. Daddy loved nice cars and had his initials engraved on them, as you can see on the door."

"*Jack Dempsey poses with Daddy and a huge Louisville Slugger bat. They used to take all kinds of promotional pictures in those days.*"

"*Comedian Charlie Chase with Daddy.*"

"Al Smith and Daddy enjoying a round of golf. Besides Daddy, quite a few well known sports celebrities supported Al Smith for President. However, Herbert Hoover still won the election."

"Notre Dame's legendary football coach Knute Rockne and Daddy, who was always willing to dress up for the photographers. Daddy really liked football and was a big Notre Dame fan."

"Lou Gehrig also supported Al Smith. Here, he and Daddy pose for photographs to show their endorsement of Smith."

"Jack Dempsey and Daddy both looking quite elegant."

"Hall of Famer Connie Mack, who at the time was the manager of the Philadelphia Athletics, and Daddy in October 1934."

"Daddy chats with Honus Wagner at the Baseball Writers Dinner on January 31, 1938."

"General Pershing gets a lesson in how to swing a bat."

"General Pershing and Daddy posing for some promotional photographs."

"Daddy salutes General Pershing."

"During the war years, Daddy was often photographed with representatives of the armed forces for bond rallies, at USO canteens and wherever else needed."

"Daddy shaking hands with another Yankee legend, Joe DiMaggio."

"Governor Thomas E. Dewey (right) of New York is greeted by Joe Louis and Daddy upon arrival at the Hotel Roosevelt on December 31, 1946, to campaign for re-election."

"Daddy meets Betty Grable on the set while he was in Hollywood to help with the filming of The Babe Ruth Story in May of 1948."

"Daddy would often dress up or do something zany to help photographers get a better picture. He was good friends with Police Commissioner Crowley of Boston and his son Arthur, and they thought that this picture would be good publicity for the department to attract young men to join the force."

"Anything for a good laugh or to create a funny and interesting picture."

"Just relaxing and catching up on the news."

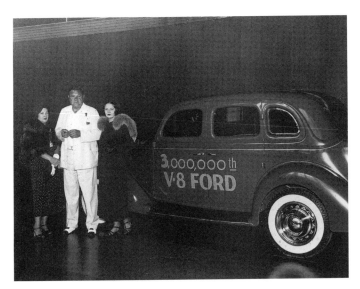

"*Mother, Daddy, and I in Michigan posing by the 3 millionth Ford produced.*"

"*Daddy just loved nice cars.*"

"*Daddy promoting a rodeo that was coming to Madison Square Garden in New York during 1928.*"

155

"Lou Gehrig joins Daddy at Dexter Park in Brooklyn, at a baseball game, to promote the rodeo."

"At a private party celebrating the opening of Steeple Chase, an amusement park at Coney Island in New York, everyone dressed up in turn of the century costumes."

"Daddy always liked to enter into the spirit of fun. Here he is chatting with me at the Steeple Chase party."

"Mother and Daddy on a bicycle built for two. (L - R) That's me and Walter Weisbecker, President and owner of West Chester Markets in New York City, looking on."

"Mother, Daddy, and I having fun at the party."

157

"We were in Paris, France, and Daddy got a big kick out of putting on a gendarme's cap and holding his club like a baseball bat."

"Whatever hat you wanted Daddy to wear for a picture he was game. Hold a tomahawk like a bat? No problem, if it makes for a good picture!"

"Santa Ruth autographs baseballs for fans."

CHAPTER 7

End of The Game

BABE RUTH'S LAST YEAR AS A YANKEE AND TWENTIETH full year in major league baseball was 1934. He had a burning desire to manage in the major leagues. In 1935, at the age of forty, he announced that his playing days were through and that he wanted to become a manager. However, for a number of reasons a managing position in the majors was not offered. In late February, Judge Emil Fuchs, owner of the Boston Braves, enticed Ruth to join the team by making him believe that the following year he may become the team's manager. Unfortunately for the Babe that never came to pass. Babe Ruth played his last major league game on May 30, 1935, for the Boston Braves and announced his retirement on June 2, 1935. From that day on he kept hoping to get a chance to manage in the major leagues, but the opportunity never came. On February 2, 1936, Babe Ruth became a charter member of the Baseball Hall of Fame.

On November 26, 1946, Babe Ruth was admitted into French Hospital in New York, and was diagnosed with throat cancer. Even though doctors performed surgery and he received radiation treatments, the cancer could not be arrested. With doctors being unable to do any more for him, Babe was released from the hospital on February 15, 1947. Subsequently, April 27 was declared "Babe Ruth Day" in every baseball park in the United States and Japan. Although too frail to don his old uniform at the time, Babe did make an appearance on that day at Yankee Stadium.

His final appearance at Yankee Stadium actually came later, on June 13, 1948, during the 25th anniversary of "The House That Ruth Built." During the celebration the Yankees also retired his uniform, number 3, and for that reason Babe put on the uniform for one last time.

On July 26, 1948, George Herman Ruth, Jr., was admitted into Memorial Hospital in New York. Subsequently, at 8:01 PM on August 16, 1948, Babe Ruth died. For two days his body lay in state at the main entrance to Yankee Stadium. Hundreds of thousands of people stood in line to pay their last respects. Babe's funeral was on August 19 at St. Patrick's Cathedral in New York. He is buried at Gate of Heaven Cemetery in Hawthorne, New York. He now rests along side of his wife Claire who was buried next to him after her death on October 25, 1976.

"Daddy was diagnosed with throat cancer in November of 1946. They never said how he got it, but he had been smoking since he was seven years old. He smoked cigarettes and pipes when he was young, and later switched to cigars."

"Even though Daddy looked frail, he still enjoyed picking up a baseball bat and hamming it up for photographers."

"Daddy golfing in Miami Beach in 1947. He loved the game of golf and I don't know what he would have done without it once he left baseball."

"Daddy recuperating in Miami Beach in 1947 with Mother on the arm of the chair and his beloved boxer Pal sitting by him."

"This card was typical of some of the elaborately decorated cards that Daddy received from his fans. His fans really loved him and were praying for him to get better."

"Daddy leaving French Hospital in New York on February 15, 1947. On the immediate left in the photograph is Agnes Merritt R. N., my uncle Hubert's wife. On the right is Charles Schwefel, a good friend and manager of the Gramercy Park

"Frank 'Home Run' Baker and Daddy at the 1947 Old Timers Game at Yankee Stadium."

BABE RUTH DAY

SEALS STADIUM AUGUST 23, 1947
San Francisco, California

"April 27, 1947, was declared 'Babe Ruth Day' for every baseball park across the United States and in Japan. This is the cover from 'Babe Ruth Day' at Seals Stadium in San Francisco."

"Daddy acknowledges the applause of the 58,379 fans at Yankee Stadium on April 27, 1947, who attended 'Babe Ruth Day' in New York."

"Daddy's address to the crowd at Yankee Stadium, on April 27, 1947, was broadcast all over by radio. He told the fans that he felt as badly as his voice sounded. He also thanked everyone for all the cards and letters that he received wishing him well. That's Mel Allen and Cardinal Spellman, of New York, behind him."

"On June 13, 1948, the New York Yankees conducted ceremonies commemorating the 25th Anniversary of Yankee Stadium, 'The House That Ruth Built.'" That same day they retired Daddy's uniform, number 3. His locker was sealed and he put on his uniform for the last time."

"Daddy acknowledges the cheers of the crowd, on June 13, 1948, as he heads toward home plate during the ceremonies at Yankee Stadium. That's Bob Feller's bat that he used as a cane. He always tried to rise to the occasion, no matter how badly he felt."

"Daddy standing by home plate in Yankee Stadium on June 13, 1948. This is a very well known and heralded photograph that was shot by Mr. Nat Fein for the 'Herald Tribune' newspaper in New York."

"The farewell speech of Daddy's at Yankee Stadium the day that they retired his uniform. Mel Allen is to the right in the photograph."

"Daddy died at 8:01 p. m. in Memorial Hospital in New York City. His coffin lay in state at the entrance to Yankee Stadium, and it was arranged so that people could pass on both sides. This was done in order to accommodate the hundreds of thousands of people, of all ages, who stood in line for hours to pay their last respects."

"Mourning fans jammed the sidewalks of New York to see Daddy's funeral procession pass."

"The funeral was on August 19, 1948, in St. Patrick's Cathedral in New York City, where Francis Cardinal Spellman recited a requiem mass. Mother was in a daze. I had to support her as we filed by the casket, with my husband Richard in the rear."

175

"A huge crowd gathered outside St. Patrick's Cathedral during Daddy's funeral. It was a dismal, rainy day, adding to the sadness of the whole thing."

"Some people brought their children to say good-bye to Daddy, who really was The Greatest Baseball Player of All Time."

"Governor Thomas E. Dewey of New York places a wreath at Daddy's memorial plaque at Yankee Stadium as Mother, Dorothy, and I look on."

"The monument at Gate of Heaven Cemetery in Hawthorne, New York where Daddy and Mother are buried."

Photo Credits

ASSOCIATED PRESS   166 top

THE BABE RUTH MUSEUM   xii, 4, 5, 6, 7, 8, 9, 10, 11, 12, 13, 14, 15, 16, 19, 20, 21, 22, 23, 24, 25, 26, 28, 29, 31, 32, 33, 35, 37, 38, 39, 40 top, 41, 49, 52, 53, 56, 57, 58, 59, 60, 61, 72, 73 bottom, 75 bottom, 76 bottom, 77 top, 78, 79 bottom, 80, 81, 82, 83 bottom, 84 bottom, 85, 86, 87, 88, 89, 90, 91, 93 top, 95, 96, 104 bottom, 105, 106 top and bottom left, 108 top left, 118, 119, 120 top left, 121 top, 125, 128 top, 130 top, 132, 134 bottom, 139, 140, 142, 144, 146 right, 148 top, 149 top and bottom left, 150, 151 bottom, 153, 154 bottom, 155 top right and bottom, 156, 158 bottom, 161, 164, 166 bottom, 170, 171, 174, 175, 176, 177, 178, 179

BETTMAN ARCHIVE   127 bottom, 129, 133 top left, 152 top

COURTESTY OF JULIA RUTH STEVENS   27, 30, 34, 36, 40 bottom, 42, 43, 44, 45, 46, 47, 48, 50, 51, 54, 62, 64, 65, 66, 67, 68, 69, 70, 71, 73 top, 74, 75 top, 76 top, 77 bottom, 79 top, 84 top, 92, 94, 98, 99, 100, 101, 102, 103, 104 top, 106 bottom right, 107, 108 top right and bottom, 109, 110, 111, 112, 113, 114, 115, 116, 135 top, 138, 143, 151 top, 152 bottom, 155 top left, 157, 158 top left and right, 162, 163, 165, 167, 168, 172

COURTESY OF LINDA TOSETTI   93 bottom, 141, 146 left

NATIONAL BASEBALL LIBRARY, COOPERSTOWN, NEW YORK   83 top, 120 top right and bottom, 121 bottom, 123, 124 bottom, 126, 127 top, 130 bottom, 131, 133 top right and bottom, 134 top, 136, 142, 147, 154 top, 169, 173

NEW YORK NEWS   124 top, 128 bottom, 135 bottom, 145, 148 bottom, 149 bottom right

UNITED PRESS INTERNATIONAL   122, 143 left